Over the
STEAMY SWAMP

OVER THE STEAMY SWAMP
A RED FOX BOOK 0 09 945992 2

First published in Great Britain by Hutchinson,
an imprint of Random House Children's Books

Hutchinson edition published 1988
This Red Fox edition published 2003

1 3 5 7 9 10 8 6 4 2

Copyright © Paul Geraghty, 1988

The right of Paul Geraghty
to be identified as the author and illustrator of this work
has been asserted in accordance with
the Copyright, Designs and Patents Act 1988.

Red Fox Books are published by Random House Children's Books.
61–63 Uxbridge Road, London W5 5SA,
a division of The Random House Group Ltd,
in Australia by Random House Australia (Pty) Ltd,
20 Alfred Street, Milsons Point, Sydney, NSW 2061, Australia,
in New Zealand by Random House New Zealand Ltd,
18 Poland Road, Glenfield, Auckland 10, New Zealand,
and in South Africa by Random House (Pty) Ltd,
Endulini, 5A Jubilee Road, Parktown 2193, South Africa

THE RANDOM HOUSE GROUP Limited Reg. No. 954009
www.kidsatrandomhouse.co.uk

A CIP catalogue record for this book is available from the British Library.

Printed and bound in China by Midas Printing Ltd

Over the STEAMY SWAMP

Paul Geraghty

RED FOX

To the Wasps: Divad Gardinium, Terenzio Fandango
and Marcus Mantis Frérém

One steamy afternoon
a mosquito flew over a swamp.

She was too tired and hungry to notice . . .

. . . a greedy dragonfly watching her.

And the dragonfly was too interested in the mosquito to notice . . .

. . . a famished frog watching him watching the mosquito.

But the frog was so excited she didn't see . . .

. . . a peckish fish watching her
watching the dragonfly
watching the mosquito.

And the fish was too busy thinking about the frog to notice . . .

. . . a hungry heron watching her
watching the frog
watching the dragonfly
watching the mosquito.

The heron was too busy thinking about dinner to notice . . .

. . . a starving snake watching him
watching the fish
watching the frog
watching the dragonfly
watching the mosquito.

But the snake was so stealthily slithering she didn't see . . .

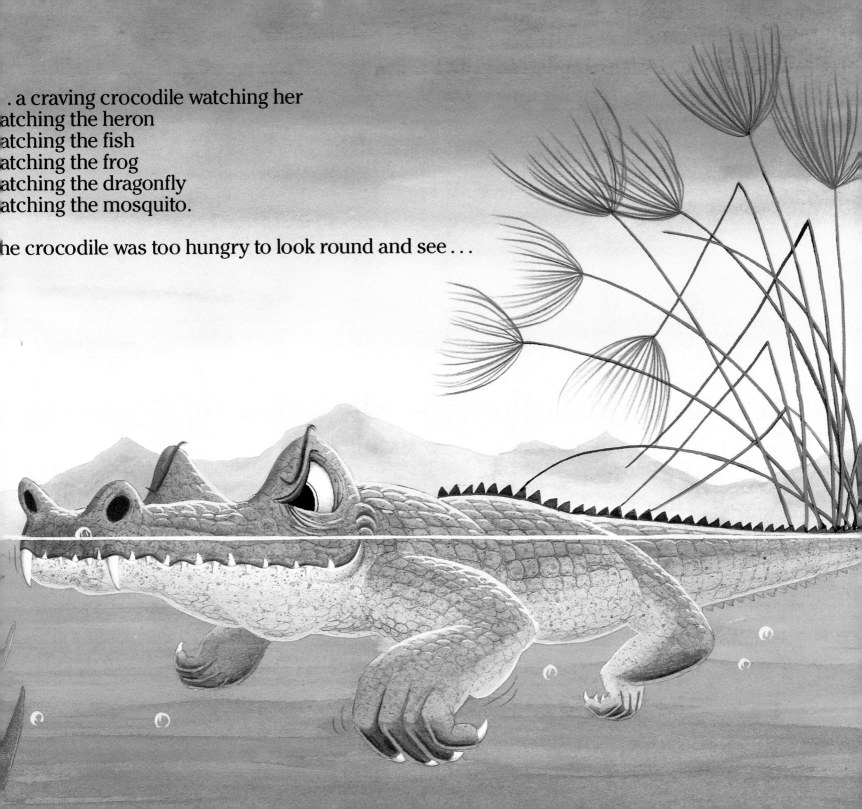

. a craving crocodile watching her
atching the heron
atching the fish
atching the frog
atching the dragonfly
atching the mosquito.

he crocodile was too hungry to look round and see . . .

. . . a hostile hunter watching him
watching the snake
watching the heron
watching the fish
watching the frog
watching the dragonfly
watching the mosquito.

And the hunter had no idea that . . .

. . . a great, big, ravenous lion was watching him
watching the crocodile
watching the snake
watching the heron
watching the fish
watching the frog
watching the dragonfly
watching the mosquito.

The great, big, ravenous lion was too busy preparing to pounce to notice . . .

. . . the mosquito
that landed on his great, big, ravenous nose and bit him.

'YEOW!' yelled the lion.

The startled snake
saw the cowering crocodile
seeing the horrified hunter
seeing the great, big, ravenous lion
that yelled, 'YEOW!'

The frightened fish saw the hysterical heron
seeing the startled snake
seeing the cowering crocodile
seeing the horrified hunter
seeing the great, big, ravenous lion that yelled, 'YEOW!'

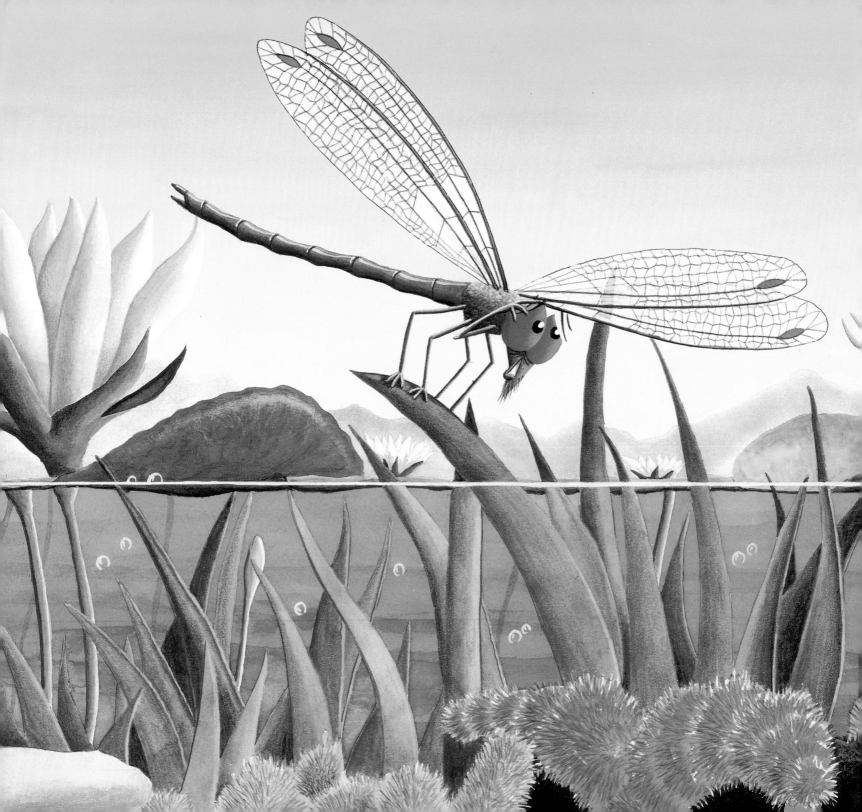

The dismayed dragonfly saw the flabbergasted frog
seeing the frightened fish
seeing the hysterical heron
seeing the startled snake
seeing the cowering crocodile
seeing the horrified hunter
seeing the great, big, ravenous lion that yelled, 'YEOW!'

Frightened creatures fled in all directions . . .

URP!

. . . and a fat mosquito flew back over the silent swamp.